SPIDERS AROUND THE WORLD

All About North American HOBO SPIDERS

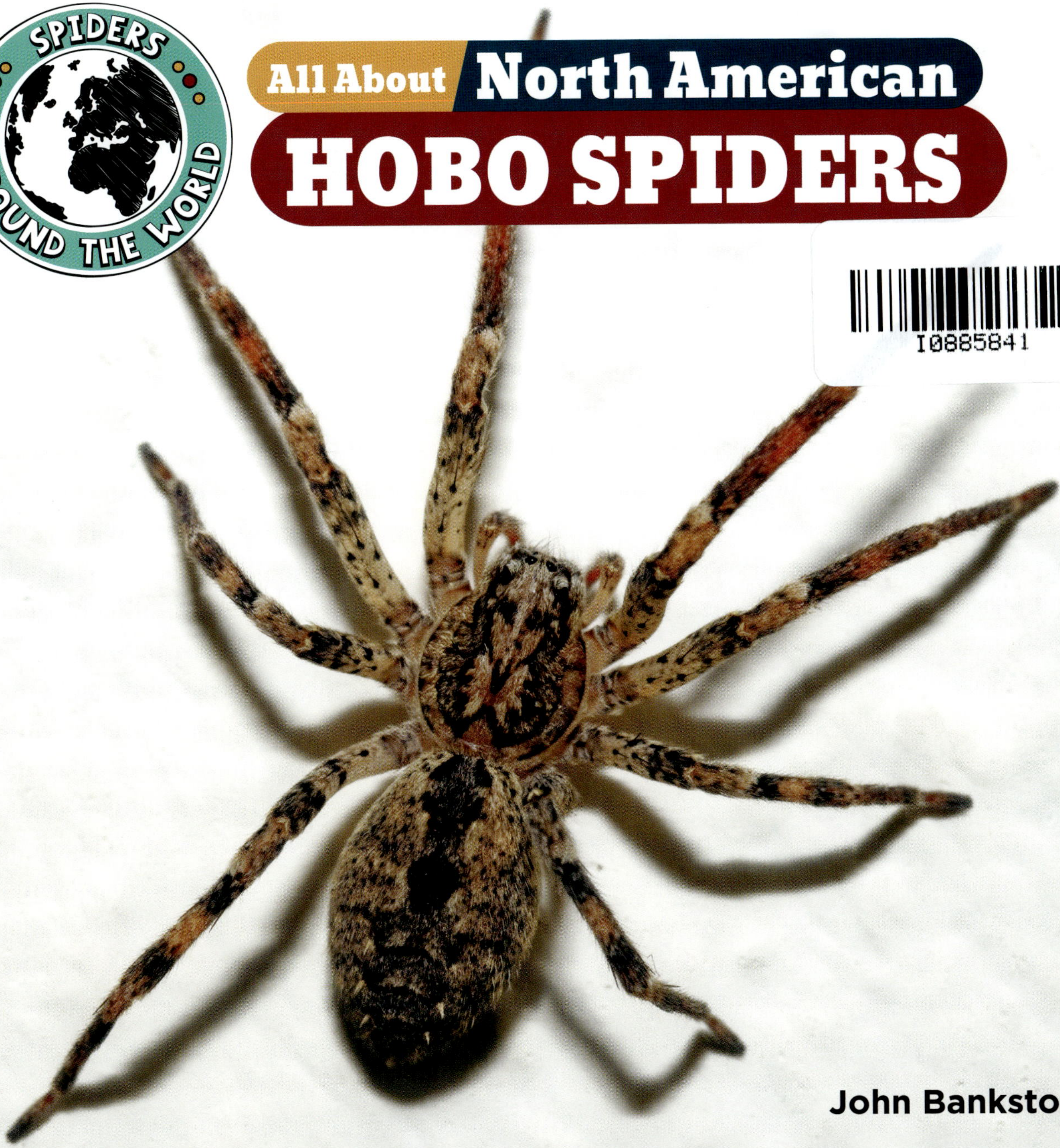

John Bankston

Mitchell Lane
PUBLISHERS
2001 SW 31st Avenue
Hallandale, FL 33009
www.mitchelllanepub.com

Little Mitchie

First Edition, 2025.

Author: John Bankston
Designer: Ed Morgan
Editor: Morgan Brody

Little Mitchie is an imprint of Mitchell Lane Publishers.

Title: All About North American Hobo Spiders
Description: Hallandale, FL : Mitchell Lane Publishers, [2025]

Series: Spiders Around the World: North America
Library bound ISBN: 978-1-68020-935-8
eBook ISBN: 978-1-68020-942-6
Paperback ISBN: 979-8-89260-162-7

Photo credits: Shutterstock

Contents

The hobo spider does not see well. This makes it hard to chase **prey**. So it builds a web. Then it waits.

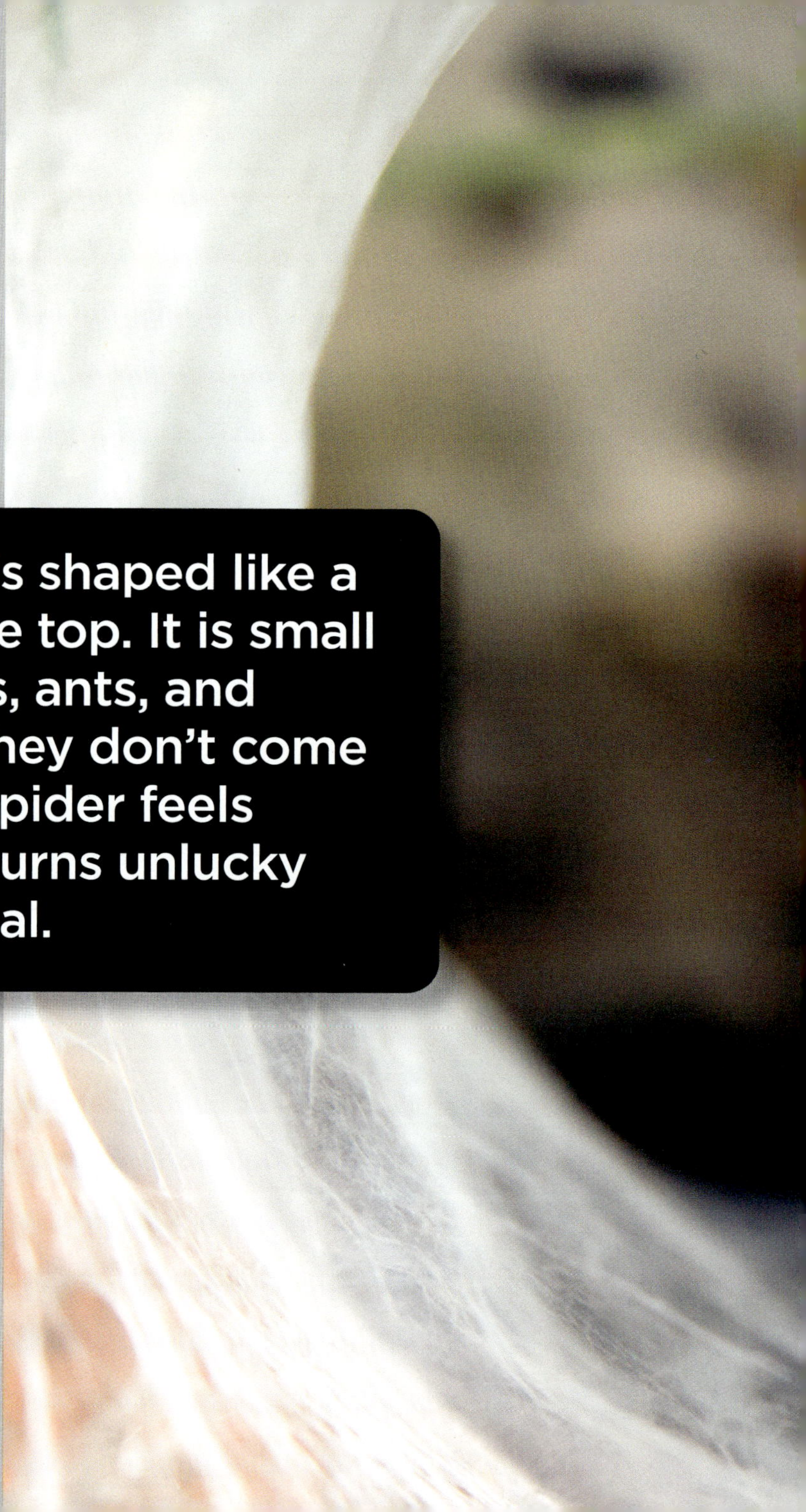

A hobo spider's web is shaped like a funnel. It is wide at the top. It is small near the bottom. Flies, ants, and other insects fall in. They don't come out. When the hobo spider feels insects hit its web, it turns unlucky bugs into a spider meal.

Large insects eat hobo spiders. The praying mantis is its biggest threat. The hobo spider can run fast when it has to.

Hobo spiders like to travel. They came to North America on boats from Europe. They covered the **continent**. They were named after working men who rode on trains.

Hobo spiders don't climb. They live their lives on the ground. These spiders hide in woodpiles. They also like rocks and basements.

They build webs in cracks and gaps. A small hole in a stone is a great place for a hobo spider home. They also hide under porches or window ledges. They might even make a web in your shoe!

Its brown color makes it very hard to see. Blending in with dirt and leaves is called **camouflage**. It is the size of a nickel. They look like many other spiders.

In the summer, males leave their webs. They are looking for female hobo spiders. The male dies after **mating**. The female lays four egg sacs. Each sac has 100 eggs. She hides them well.

Hobo spiders use **venom** to kill. They hardly ever bite people. Hobo spiders are more scared of us than we are of them.

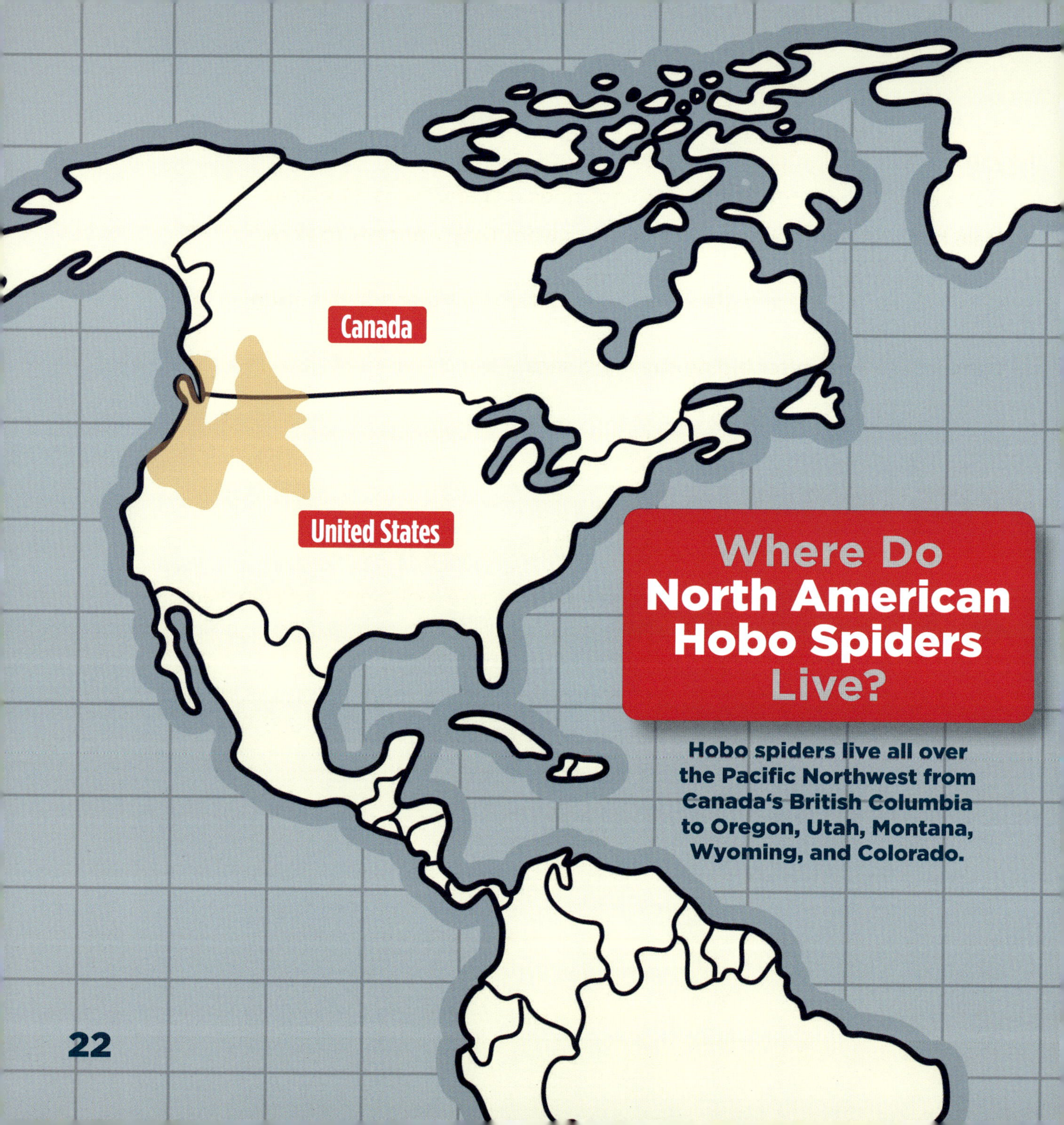

Where Do **North American Hobo Spiders** Live?

Hobo spiders live all over the Pacific Northwest from Canada's British Columbia to Oregon, Utah, Montana, Wyoming, and Colorado.

Interesting **Facts**

- Hobo spiders get around by "hitching" rides on cars, trains, or planes.
- Male hobo spiders knock on the female's web. They want her to know they are friendly.
- Hobo spider bites are *not* deadly. People bitten by other spiders often blame the hobo.
- Females die soon after hiding their egg sacs.
- Hobo spider webs are not sticky.

Parts of a North American Hobo Spider

Spiders are not insects. They are **arachnids**. They have eight legs and spin webs.

Abdomen
Yellow marks on its back let you know this is a hobo spider.

Eyes
These spiders have eight eyes. They have four on one side of their head and four on the other.

Legs
Very hairy with feet made for web climbing.

Teeth
Few spiders have more than five teeth. The hobo spider can have eight!

Glossary

abdomen (ab-DOE-men)
Place where the stomach is located

arachnid (a-rack-NID)
An eight-legged creature without antenna

camouflage (cam-o-FLAJE)
When an animal's color helps it blend in and hide

continent (con-TIN-ent)
Huge land mass surrounded by water.

mating (MAYT-ing)
When male and females of the same **species** come together to create offspring

prey (pray)
Insect or other creature hunted for food

species (speesh-EEZs)
Living things that are very similar

venom (ven-OM)
A dangerous liquid that is injected by an animal

Further Reading

All Things Spiders For Kids: Filled With Plenty of Facts, Photos, and Fun to Learn all About Spiders. Berlin, Germany: Admore Publishing, 2022.

Sovak, Jan. *Learning About Spiders.* Mineola, NY: Dover, 2019.

London, Martha. *Spiders*. Newburyport, MA: Focus Readers, 2020.

On the Internet

Discover some interesting facts about the Hobo Spider on A to Z animals:
https://a-z-animals.com/animals/hobo-spider/

Find out more about the Hobo Spider on Animal Corner:
https://animalcorner.org/animals/hobo-spider/

See lots of pictures of the Hobo Spider:
https://bugguide.net/node/view/31446/bgimage

This video from Montana State University talks about hobo spiders in the home:
https://www.youtube.com/watch?v=daewM5FbYjM

Index